CRAFT HAPPY

Paper Crafting
with Flowers

Craft Happy: Paper Crafting with Flowers
Copyright © 2013 by Editions de Paris Inc.

Published in English in 2013 by:
Harper Design
An Imprint of HarperCollins*Publishers*
10 East 53rd Street
New York, NY 10022
Tel (212) 207-7000
harperdesign@harpercollins.com
www.harpercollins.com

Distributed throughout the world by:
HarperCollins*Publishers*
10 East 53rd Street
New York, NY 10022

This book was originally published in Japanese as *Paper Crafts Overflowing with Flower*s.
Japanese edition © 2011 by Editions de Paris Inc.
English translation rights arranged with Editions de Paris Inc. through ricorico llc.
info@editionsdeparis.com
www.editionsdeparis.com

Interior design: Chigusa Hiraki, Andrew Pothecary (forbidden colour)
Photography: Nao Shimizu
Styling: Tomoe Ito
Writing: Mayumi Akagi
Illustration: Chihiro Yoshii
Flower motifs and patterns: Kanako Uno
Planning and editing: Aya Nagaoka, Miyuki Matsuda (Editions de Paris)
Styling cooperation: Orné de Feuilles, AWABEES
Translation: Timothy Ryan Miller, TranNet KK
Chief Editor and Production Manager: Aki Ueda (ricorico)

Library of Congress Control Number: 2012951247

ISBN: 978-0-06224765-0

Printed in China
First printing, 2013

CRAFT HAPPY
Paper Crafting
with Flowers

PROLOGUE

How do you feel when you receive a bouquet of gorgeous flowers? First you are a bit surprised, and then you are enveloped by a warm feeling of happiness.

Flowers possess this kind of wonderful power.

A colorful, elegant craft that's full of flowers also makes a touching gift for significant others, family members, and friends—a person you know well or one you're just getting close with.

In this book, we have a magnificent collection of handmade craft items that embrace floral designs. They've been made using romantic motifs and easily accessible paper. They can be accented with pressed flowers or have flowers painted, collaged, or sewn on.

The projects were made by four groups of talented artists and each one was carefully developed. The pattern paper in the back of the book will allow you to start crafting right away. Be ready though, if you gift one of the projects inside you will surely get a smile, perhaps even a hug, from the delighted recipient.

CONTENTS

Essential Tools
CONVENIENT TOOLS FOR MAKING PAPER CRAFTS

A **Cutter knife** Essential for cutting paper and creating cut designs.

B **Scissors** Useful when cutting detailed motifs.

C **Single hole punch** Comes in handy when punching holes in tags and binding paper.

D **Eyeleteer** A tool for punching holes when sewing paper with a thread.

E **Glue stick/Spray glue** A glue stick is easy to use and you will usually be fine using one. Spray glues are useful when you need to work quickly or when you are gluing onto a bumpy surface.

F **Liquid glue** For corsages and other small parts. Use on any material other than paper.

G **Stamps** It's nice to have a full set of alphabet and other character stamps.

H **Pens/Pencils** For stenciling and writing messages.

I **Ruler** For accurate length measurements and cutting straight lines.

J **Brushes/Paints** Apply colors to your liking to make your own original paper.

K **Tweezers** For handling small, delicate objects like pressed flowers and beads.

L **Sewing kit** Use for stitching and sewing small parts together.

8

Flower Materials: Tips and Tricks
FROM CORSAGES AND PRESSED FLOWERS TO MASKING TAPE

A **Floral paper** You can buy this or make a color copy of an antique fabric.

B **Masking tape** Delicate flower patterns or lace patterns are particularly lovely.

C **Stickers** Collect plenty from floral-theme to actual pressed-flower stickers.

D **Paper corsage** Very affective, you can brighten any design by adding just a single corsage.

E **Ribbon/Lace** There are loads of lovely varieties from floral-patterned to flower-embroidered.

F **Buttons** Use to accent a collage for a three-dimensional effect.

G **Flower cabochons** Add to a collage to make a more bountiful effect.

H **Vintage flower motifs** To add a little flair.

I **Pressed flowers/Dried flowers** Use real flowers to create a more elegant and delicate craft.

The other tools required for each project are indicated in its "What you will need" section.

CHAPTER 1

Flowery Gift Cards

It can be tough to find the right words to write to a friend or family member. However, there's no need to over-think it. Send a handmade card delicately accented with your recipient's favorite flowers. The sentiment will be clear.

PROJECT 1
New Year's Card with Wild Flowers

Creator: Aya Nagaoka

A NEW YEAR'S GREETING SPELLED OUT WITH STICKERS AND SEALED WITH PRESSED FLOWERS. WITH ITS MOSS GREEN STRIPES, THIS CARD PORTRAYS AN IMAGE OF FLOWERS BLOOMING IN A FIELD.

WHAT YOU WILL NEED:

- *Drawing paper*
- *Alphabet and pressed-flower stickers*
- *Patterned paper / Lace paper / Old stamps / Labels*
- *Lace / Buttons / Charms*
- *Cutter knife / Cutting mat / Ruler / Glue / Stamps*

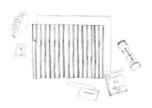

1 Cut a piece of drawing paper to postcard size, and then affix a piece of patterned paper. Create a collage using scraps of lace paper, antique stamps, labels, and the like. Avoid loud colors so that the flowers will stand out.

2 Spell out your message using alphabet pressed-flower stickers and stamps. The card above includes the French New Year's greeting "BONNE ANNÉE." Finally, add on a few buttons or other accents.

THIS CARD IS LIGHTLY
SCENTED WITH LAVENDER
AS IF LACED WITH FRESH AIR
FROM THE COUNTRYSIDE,
TRANSPORTING ITS RECIPIENT
TO THE PROVENCE REGION IN
THE SOUTH OF FRANCE. USE
IT TO ADD A SUMMERY FEEL
TO YOUR GREETING.

PROJECT 2

Lavender-Scented Summer Card

Creator: Ananö

WHAT YOU WILL NEED:

- *Postcard*
- *Glassine paper / Lace paper / Labels*
- *Dried lavender / Lavender perfume / Lace*
- *Needle / Silver thread*
- *Glue / Pencil*

1. Affix glassine paper or lace paper to an antique postcard, and then decorate the edge of the postcard with lace. Use silver thread to attach the lace for an attractive stitching accent.

2. Attach two or three stalks of dried lavender with a label on which you can write a message. Finally, spray the card with some lavender fragrance. Enclose your card in an envelope made of a translucent paper such as glassine paper.

PROJECT 3

Flower Bouquet
Birthday Card

Creator: Saji

THIS BIRTHDAY CARD'S VARIOUS SHADES OF PURPLE CREATE AN ELEGANT EFFECT. THE GORGEOUS BOUQUET OF FLOWERS WILL BLOOM FOREVER SINCE IT'S MADE OF A COLLECTION OF CUTOUT FLOWERS. TRY DELIVERING THE CARD WITH A REAL BOUQUET OF MATCHING FLOWERS TO TRULY DELIGHT YOUR FRIEND OR LOVED ONE.

 WHAT YOU WILL NEED:

- *Drawing paper*
- *Ribbon / Lace / Leather / Beads*
- *Scissors / Cutter knife / Cutting mat / Ruler / Glue / Brush / Paints / Tweezers*

Decorate the center of the flowers with leather cut into circles and beads, paying attention to the balance between the three-dimensional effect of the flowers and the colors.

1 Cut a piece of drawing paper into an 8 × 5 inches rectangle, and color the entire piece with paint. A lovely pearl white was used in the featured card. Once the paint has dried, glue on lace to create a frame around the four edges.

2 Next, make the cutout flowers. Use the templates to cut out the flowers from purple-colored drawing paper. Prepare stems using green-colored drawing paper. Affix the stems first, followed by the flowers.

3 Decorate your card with plenty of the cutout flowers. Affix a bow made with ribbon on top of the stems so that it appears to bundle the flowers together. Write a "Happy Birthday" message in the surrounding blank area.

Tip: You can add leather to the center of the flowers and pop the the petals out to create a 3-D effect.

Template for flower motif cutout design: enlarge by 150%

PROJECT 4

Mini Rose Card Made with Masking Tape

Creator: Aya Nagaoka

WHEN SENDING GREETINGS FOR MOTHER'S DAY OR JUST AN ORDINARY THANK-YOU TO A CLOSE FRIEND, IT'S NICE TO SPEND A LITTLE EXTRA TIME TO MAKE A HEARTFELT CARD. HOW ABOUT CREATING A MINIATURE ROSE WITH MASKING TAPE AND LETTING IT BLOOM GRACEFULLY ON ONE CORNER OF YOUR CARD?

WHAT YOU WILL NEED:

- *Postcard*
- *Flower-patterned masking tape*
- *Old stamps / Labels / Bird motifs*
- *Artificial leaves / Lace / Pearl beads*
- *Glue / Stamps*

1 First make your miniature rose. Tear off an 8–9 inch piece of masking tape, and fold down from the top about $^1/_3$ of the width, as shown in the illustration. In this example, a $^5/_8$-inch wide masking tape was used.

2 Now roll up the masking tape strip starting at one end. While gripping the lower portion as if to squeeze it, gather the masking tape randomly. When you have finished rolling the entire strip, fasten the bottom with a small piece of cut tape. This should create the look of bunched petals.

3 Make about five miniature roses. Affix them and real leaves to the corner of an antique postcard. You can achieve a three-dimensional effect by clustering the flowers together when affixing them.

4 Using stamps, write the French "MERCI" meaning "thank you" on a label and affix it to the card. Finish off your card with a collage of antique stamps, bird motifs, lace, pearl beads, or the like.

You can also take a simple mini-card and turn it into a gorgeous tag by adorning it with a few masking tape miniature roses.

THIS CARD USES DRIED ROSES, CHIFFON, AND TWO TYPES OF
FLOWER PETALS TO FASHION A "FLOWER SHOWER" OF SORTS,
GIVING SHAPE TO YOUR HEARTFELT CONGRATULATIONS. SEND
WISHES OF HAPPINESS TO THAT SPECIAL COUPLE WITH A
WHITE CARD THAT'S AS PURE AS THE BRIDE'S DRESS.

WHAT YOU WILL NEED:
- *Thick paper / Thin paper*
- *Lace paper*
- *Dried roses / Chiffon cloth / Ribbon / Lace / Gold thread*
- *Scissors / Cutter knife / Cutting mat / Ruler / Glue / Sealing stamps / Sealing wax / Pens*

1 Cut a piece of thick paper into a 7 3/4 x 5 3/4 inches rectangle, and then fold it in half leaving an extra 3/8 inch at one end. Write a message on the front of the card and attach lace on the front edge. Decorate the front with dried rose petals and thin fabric cut into the shape of flower petals.

2 Prepare a card insert by cutting a piece of thin paper into a 6 3/4 x 5 3/8 inches rectangle and folding it in half. Write a message on the insert, and decorate it with flower petals and lace paper. Place the card insert into the card and bind them with a gold thread.

3 Affix several flower petals to a strip of ribbon as shown in the illustration. Attach one end of the ribbon to the front of the card with sealing wax, and then close the card by wrapping it with the ribbon.

You can enclose your white card in a pale blue envelope to give the bride her "something blue." Decorate the envelope with matching flower petals.

PROJECT 6

Invitation with Alice's Tea Party Theme

Creator: les deux

Wouldn't you love to welcome your friends to a special event with this adorable box card? When your guests open the lid of this tiny, romantic flower-patterned box, they will be delighted to find an invitation to a tea party overflowing with flowers. Your guests may even be greeted by a tiny figurine peeking out of this whimsical invitation. This lovely card will surely entice your guests to your small gathering, where you can entertain them with sweet handmade cakes and delicious tea.

1 Cut a piece of thick paper using the template below. Use the back of a cutter knife to put creases for folding along the dashed lines on the template. Use the template again to cut a piece of patterned paper, and glue it onto the thick paper.

2 Assemble the box along the creases you made in step one. To make a sturdy box, securely affix the overlap portions using a strong double-sided tape.

3 Cut a piece of colored paper to the size of the lid of the box from step two, and glue it onto the inside of the lid. Gather up a piece of thin fabric and affix it to the lid in a flowing fashion, and then decorate the lid with a string of pearl beads.

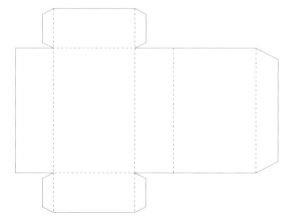

Box template: enlarge by 330% (Finished size: 3 x 4⁵/₁₆ x 1⁵/₁₆ inches)

WHAT YOU WILL NEED:

- *Thick paper*
- *Patterned paper / Colored paper*
- *Corsage / Mini ceramic doll / Cloth / Ribbon / Buttons / Pearl beads*
- *Needle / Thread / Eyeleteer*
- *Cutter knife / Cutting mat / Ruler / Glue / Double-faced tape / Pens*

4 Fill up the box with floral corsages, a miniature doll, and the like. Try selecting your flowers to match the season, and adding a few interesting treats like small fruits, nuts, even a tea bag with a delicious smell.

5 Sew a button onto the flap of the lid with thread. Use an eyeleteer to punch holes for passing your needle when sewing on the button. Tie the end of a strand of ribbon to the base of the button.

6 Put a message on the inside of the lid. If you can't fit the whole message, you can also put a mini-card into the box. Close the lid and wrap up the box with the ribbon.

This box is also the perfect size for putting in a small present. Your recipient will surely be filled with anticipation to find out what's inside, just like searching for a treasure among a field of flowers.

PROJECT 7

Springtime Tulips
Stationery Set

Creator: Aya Nagaoka

"WOULD YOU LIKE TO ACCOMPANY ME ON AN OUTING TO WELCOME THE ARRIVAL OF SPRING?" THIS HANDMADE STATIONARY IS PERFECT FOR SUCH AN INVITATION. FEATURING A COLLAGE OF TULIPS AND MARGUERITE DAISIES ON COOL-MINT GREEN PAPER, IT DELIVERS A WARM MESSAGE ON THE SPRINGTIME WINDS.

 WHAT YOU WILL NEED:

- *Drawing paper / Envelope (for template)*
- *Newspaper / Cellophane sheet*

- *Ribbon / Lace*
- *Scissors / Cutter knife / Cutting mat / Ruler / Glue / Brush / Paints / Tweezers*

You can give your tulips depth by using similar shades of colored paper for the petals, and then slightly overlapping each top petal with the one below it.

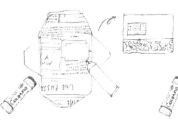

1 First make the envelope. Open up any envelope you have on hand and use it as a template to cut an envelope from a piece of drawing paper. Color the entire paper mint green with paint, and let it dry thoroughly.

2 Affix a piece of newspaper to the inside of the envelope. Cut out a window on the envelope, and attach a piece of cellophane cut just bigger than the window. Assemble the envelope with glue. Attach lace to its front.

3 Using the templates below, cut a piece of colored drawing paper into the flower parts. Attach the flowers to the envelope to surround the window.

4 Now create the letter paper. Cut a piece of drawing paper so that it will fit snugly into the envelope when folded in half. Decorate it with cutout flowers, and add some butterfly cutouts as well. Use ribbon and lace for finishing touches.

*Templates for the tulips, marguerite daisies, and butterflies ** Feel free to enlarge the templates as needed to match the final size of your stationery.*

PROJECT 8

Moving Congratulations Card Overflowing with Flowers

Creator: Aya Nagaoka

FLORAL WALLPAPER, FLOWERS IN A FRAME, A HUGE FLOWER BASKET—THIS CARD CREATES A SPACE THAT FEELS LIKE ENTERING A DOLLHOUSE OVERFLOWING WITH FLOWERS. GIFT YOUR RECENTLY RELOCATED FRIENDS WITH AN IDEAL ROOM FILLED WITH YOUR WELL WISHES FOR THEIR NEW LIFE.

WHAT YOU WILL NEED:

- *Thick paper*
- *Flower-patterned paper / Floral-theme stickers*
- *Paper corsage*
- *Patterned paper / Colored paper / Furniture motifs*
- *Miniature dollhouse frame / Miniature shoes / Antique key / Ribbon*
- *Scissors / Cutter knife / Cutting mat / Ruler / Glue / Foam sheet / Stamps*

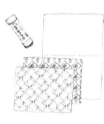

1. Cut a piece of thick paper into an 8 ^{3}/4 x 6 ^{1}/2 inches rectangle. Fold it in half once and then open it back up. Affix a floral-theme paper that resembles wallpaper on one side, and then affix a patterned paper that resembles flooring on the other side.

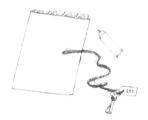

2. Copy furniture motifs from an illustration book or the like onto colored drawing paper and then cut them out. Give the furniture cutouts a three-dimensional effect by affixing pieces of a foam sheet cut into narrow strips onto the back of each one.

3. Attach the cutouts to the card. Arrange them as the furniture might be arranged in a real room. Then add paper corsages and miniature frames in a three-dimensional collage, so that the room comes to life like a real dollhouse.

4. Affix ribbon to the front of the card and wrap the ribbon around the card to close it. Tie an antique key and a tag stamped with a room number on the end of the ribbon.

You can add life to your finished cards just by adding a mini-frame.

PROJECT 9
Floral Bon Voyage
Message Card
Creator: les deux

ACCENTED WITH A CUTE SQUIRREL MOTIF ALONG WITH
PRESERVED FLOWERS AND PRESSED-FLOWER STICKERS, THIS
CARD LOOKS AS IF IT JUMPED RIGHT OUT OF THE FOREST!
FILL IT WITH MESSAGES FROM THE RECIPIENT'S CLOSEST
FRIENDS, AND SHE IS SURE TO TREASURE THIS CARD FOREVER.

WHAT YOU WILL NEED:

- *Colored drawing paper*
- *Flower-patterned masking tape / Pressed-flower stickers*
- *White paper (for the photocopy) /*
  Lace paper / Labels / Squirrel motif
- *Preserved flowers / Ribbon*
- *Scissors / Cutter knife / Cutting mat / Ruler / Glue /*
  Pens / Tweezers

1 Cut a piece of colored drawing paper into an 8¹/₄ x 8¹/₄ inches square. Use the pattern below to cut wave designs along each of the four sides and a cutout design at each corner. Affix this onto another piece of colored drawing paper that is cut into a slightly larger square.

2 In the center of the paper, affix lace paper, a label, and preserved hydrangeas. Copy a squirrel motif from an illustration book or the like, and then cut it out and add it to your arrangement by gluing only the bottom portion of the motif onto the paper.

3 Now, affix pressed-flower stickers or motifs cut out from patterned masking tape to the card. Decorate the top of the card with a bow made from ribbon, and write your messages in the blank spaces.

Template for flower motif cutout design: enlarge by 200%

FEATURING A COLORFUL WREATH AND A SWINGING WHITE BIRDCAGE, THIS CARD EVOKES CHRISTMAS AT A CHURCH IN EUROPE. IT IS SO LOVELY THAT IT CAN EVEN BE USED AS A DECORATIVE PIECE IN YOUR HOME. THE TINY BIRD PERCHED ON THE TREE BRANCH IS SURE TO DELIVER JOY TO YOUR LOVED ONES AT CHRISTMAS.

WHAT YOU WILL NEED:

- *Drawing paper / Mini-card*
- *Colored drawing paper / Flower motifs*
- *Wreath (10" in diameter, 7" in inside diameter) / Bird motif / Nut motifs / Plumes / Ribbon / String*
- *Scissors / Cutter knife / Cutting mat / Ruler / Glue / Tape / Pens*

Tape a piece of string suited to your mini-card to the ceiling of the birdcage so that the cage hangs down.

1 First make the birdcage. Cut a piece of drawing paper into four strips, each measuring 12 x ³⁄₈ inches. Affix three of the strips together at their centers as shown in the above illustration. Form the remaining strips into a ring, and then affix the edges of the three strips to the ring as shown above.

2 Cut holly leaves from colored drawing paper. Write your greetings on the leaves and then affix them to an antique mini-card. Punch a hole into the top of the card, insert a piece of string, and tie the card onto the cage.

3 Decorate your wreath by sticking in flower and fruit motifs, feathers, and the like, using Christmas colors for the color scheme. Attach your bird so that it looks like it's perched on the wreath.

4 Attach the birdcage to the wreath. Cut a 2³⁄₄ x ³⁄₈ inches strip from a piece of drawing paper and make it into a ring, then attach the ring to the top of the bird cage. Pass a long strand of ribbon through the ring and tie it to the wreath.

Small birds, butterflies, mushrooms, fruits, leaves—any of these motifs featuring friends of the flowers in the natural world work wonderfully when making floral cards.

CHAPTER 2

Flowery Gift Wrapping

When you want to delicately wrap a
present with just a bit of love, how
about making that extra effort to create
beautiful wrapping paper yourself?
A handmade gift wrap effortlessly
decorated with flowers will surely bring
you closer to your recipient. That's
right, the wrapping is also an essential
part of your precious gift.

PROJECT 11

Lovely Viola
Gift Tag

Creator: Aya Nagaoka

This gift tag is like an ornament brought to life with a collage of lovely pressed violas. Since the tag is fully covered with glassine paper, it will keep beautifully. You can even give this tag as a bookmark.

What you will need:

- *Thick paper*
- *Floral-theme stickers / Pressed flowers*
- *Clippings from an old book / Glassine paper / Lace paper / Labels*
- *Ribbon / Lace / Eyelet*
- *Needle / Embroidery thread / Eyeleteer*
- *Cutter knife / Cutting mat / Ruler / Hole punch / Glue / Spray glue / Pencils / Tweezers*

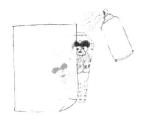

1. Cut out a piece of paper from an old book and affix it to a piece of thick paper, and then cut it to a $5^3/4$ x $2^1/2$ inches rectangle. Remove the corners so that it looks like a tag. Decorate the tag with a collage of pressed flowers, lace paper, and the like.

2. Cover the entire tag with a piece of glassine paper that is cut considerably larger than the tag. It is recommended to coat the tag evenly with a spray glue to affix the glassine paper. Once dry, cut off any excess portions of the glassine paper.

3. Next, embroider the tag. Draw a guideline of your motif with a pencil, and then poke needle holes with an eyeleteer and sew by passing the needle through the holes. In the tag shown on the opposite page, a letter was stitched using cross-stitching.

4. Decorate the tag with lace. You can create a feminine touch by affixing lace across the bottom edge like a frill. Punch a hole at the top of the tag with a single hole punch, insert a metallic eyelet, and finish it off with a piece of ribbon.

Pressed flowers are very useful for wrapping and collages. You can make your own by picking fresh flowers, or you can buy them from a specialty store. They can be fragile, so use a pair of tweezers when handling them.

This exquisite corsage was created by crafting a looped ribbon design like that found on a flower shop bouquet using paper and ribbon. Try adding this corsage onto a simple paper bag or attaching it directly to a gift.

What you will need:

- *Drawing paper*
- *Ribbons (use 2–3 fabrics with different colors or designs and made from materials such as suede and satin) / Lace / Tulle*
- *Scissors / Glue / Brush / Paints / Clips*
- *Needle / Embroidery thread / Eyeleteer*
- *Cutter knife / Cutting mat / Ruler / Hole punch / Glue / Spray glue / Pencils / Tweezers*

1 Cut about ten strips, each 4³/₄ inches in length, from a piece of drawing paper, then color them with paint. The strips should be of various widths from ¹/₄–³/₄ inch and several similar colors.

2 Curl the strips into loop shapes and bundle them together in a bouquet. Try adding in ribbon and tulle similarly cut into lengths of 4³/₄ inches. Secure the bundled portion with an adhesive, and hold with a clip until dry.

3 Affix a piece of drawing paper or ribbon cut into a long strip onto the bundled portion and let it hang. Next, decorate the corsage with a strip of wide lace tied into a bow. Finally, use a long strand of ribbon to wrap your corsage and tie it onto a gift.

You can create a much more bountiful effect that's perfect for a celebration just by changing the colors and materials you use, such as adding reds and golds or incorporating raffia. Try it on a box or wine bottle.

PROJECT 13

Blooming Flower Accessory Wrapping

Creator: Ananö

FOR A SMALL PRESENT, SUCH AS A RING, BROOCH, OR OTHER SOUVENIR, YOU CAN ENHANCE THE ELEMENT OF SURPRISE WITH CREATIVE WRAPPING. HOW ABOUT CREATING A SINGLE FLOWER WITH GATHERED PAPER? THIS WRAPPING EXPRESSES THE AIRY NUANCE OF FLOWER PETALS BY USING A VERY THIN PAPER.

WHAT YOU WILL NEED:

- *Thin paper*
- *Old stamps / Labels*
- *Center of a faux flower / Lace / String*
- *Scissors / Tape / Sealing stamps / Sealing wax*
- *Cutter knife / Cutting mat / Ruler / Hole punch / Glue / Spray glue / Pencils / Tweezers*

1 Place your gift on top of a piece of thin paper, and fold the paper in thirds, so as to wrap up the gift from both sides. Fold in half from top to bottom. For the thin paper, select a size with which you can wrap your gift while leaving a great deal leftover to create a blooming effect.

2 Gather the thin paper about $1^1/_4$–$1^5/_8$ inches from the top. Insert the center of a faux flower into the center of the gathered portion and adhere it with tape. Tie up the gathered portion with a strand of lace or string. Open up the top portion to create a blooming flower effect.

3 Finish by using an old stamp or sealing wax to affix the lace or string. By selecting different sizes of thin paper, you can change the volume of the flower portion, thereby changing the overall effect of the wrapping.

Try creating by stacking different colored sheets of thin paper on top of each other to increase the volume of the flower and give more life to the flower petals.

PROJECT 14

White Hydrangea Paper Bag

Creator: Ananö

Your recipient will want to keep this decorative paper bag forever. It's beautiful enough to create a piece of art just by hanging it on a wall in your room. Send this bag to a special girlfriend who would look lovely carrying a white hydrangea.

What you will need:

- *Plain paper bag / Thick paper / Mini-card*
- *Flower-patterned masking tape / Pressed-flower stickers (circular type)*
- *Clippings from an old book / Lace paper / Old stamps*
- *Preserved flowers / Lace / String / Brads*
- *Needle / Thread / Eyeleteer*
- *Scissors / Cutter knife / Cutting mat / Ruler / Glue / Tape / Sealing stamps / Sealing wax*

1 Cut a piece of thick paper into a rectangle having a width of 2 3/8 inches and a length that is slightly longer than the length of the base of your paper bag. Cover the entire rectangle with masking tape, and then fold it in half. This will become the base of your paper bag.

2 Horizontally cut off the base of the paper bag. Insert the paper bag into the folded rectangle and attach it with glue. Punch a hole with an eyeleteer about 1/4 inch from the bottom and sew the base to the paper bag with thread to strengthen it.

3 Wrap the masking tape around the handles of the paper bag. Create a collage on the front of the paper bag using a preserved hydrangea, cutouts from an antique book, vintage stamps, and the like.

4 Attach a brad to the upper part of the front of the paper bag and affix the end of a piece of string to the back of the bag with tape, so as to close the bag. Tie mini-cards collaged with pressed flower stickers and the like to the loose ends of the string.

The possibilities are endless when designing mini-cards. Try covering the entire front of the card with masking tape or decorating it with pressed-flower stickers.

PROJECT 15

Pressed-Flower Envelope

Creator: les deux

WRAP UP YOUR CONGRATULATIONS WITH THIS GORGEOUS GIFT ENVELOPE. THE FOCAL POINT OF THIS ENVELOPE IS THE PARTIALLY THREE-DIMENSIONAL BOUQUET CREATED WITH A MIXTURE OF REAL PRESSED FLOWERS AND CUTOUT PRESSED FLOWERS.

Fold the bottom so that it rests on top when stacked over the other fold.

The finished size of the envelope will be 7 x 4³/₄ inches so that a monetary gift can be inserted without being folded.

WHAT YOU WILL NEED:

- *Colored drawing paper*
- *Flower-patterned masking tape*
- *Pressed flowers*
- *Colored paper / White paper (for the photocopy)*
- *Ribbon / String*
- *Scissors / Cutter knife / Cutting mat / Ruler / Glue*

1 Cut a piece of colored drawing paper into a 15 x 11 inches rectangle. Create a border along one edge by affixing masking tape and a piece of colored paper cut into a wave pattern. Fold the paper into thirds, leaving an extra ³/₈ inch on one side. Put in your gift, and then fold over the top and bottom.

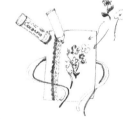

2 Create a bouquet on the front of the envelope using pressed flowers and cutouts of color-copied pressed flowers. Use layered ribbon and lace to tie the envelope.

THIS TINY ENVELOPE IS USEFUL FOR
GIVING A SMALL THANK-YOU GIFT. WITH
ITS CHIC FLORAL PATTERN AND NEAT
PRESSED FLOWERS, YOU CAN ALSO USE
THIS ENVELOPE TO ADD A SOPHISTICATED
TOUCH TO A SMALL PRESENT.

PROJECT 16

Envelope of Tiny Flowers

Creator: Aya Nagaoka

WHAT YOU WILL NEED:

- *Colored drawing paper / Small paper envelope (for template)*
- *Flower-patterned paper*
- *Flower-patterned masking tape*
- *Pressed flowers stickers*
- *Pressed flowers*
- *Lace papers / Old stamps*
- *Lace / String*
- *Cutter knife / Cutting mat / Ruler / Glue / Sealing stamps / Sealing wax*

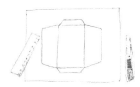

1. Open a small envelope to use as a template. Cut a piece of paper that you have chosen for your small envelope using the template, and then fold it up into an envelope and seal it with glue. The above picture features two envelopes, one with a floral pattern and one plain.

2. Add accents to the floral-patterned envelope by affixing pressed-flower stickers or antique stamps. For the plain envelope, affix a pressed flower and lace paper. Wrap it with a string, then seal it with sealing wax.

PROJECT 17

Rose-Theme Dessert Toothpicks

Creator: Saji

THESE SWEETS ARE BLOOMING WITH A GARDEN OF COLORFUL ROSES. THE TOOTHPICKS ARE PERFECT FOR FINGER FOODS AT A PARTY, AS WELL AS DECORATING SWEET TREATS TO SHARE WITH YOUR FRIENDS. YOUR GUESTS WILL HAVE SO MUCH FUN DECIDING WHICH ONE TO CHOOSE.

Cut off the base corners so that the edge of folded part on the back side of the flag cannot be seen from the front when the paper is wrapped around the toothpick.

WHAT YOU WILL NEED:

- *Colored drawing paper*
- *Cloth / Lace / Beads / Toothpicks*
- *Scissors / Glue / Brush / Paints / Tweezers*

1. Cut a piece of drawing paper into an isosceles triangle with a base of $1\frac{7}{8}$ inches and a height of $2\frac{1}{4}$ inches, then color the triangle with paint. Affix fabric to the backside, and cut off the base corners diagonally. For guidance, see the cut of the light pink paper on the toothpick in the mug above.

2. Wrap the triangle onto a toothpick and attach it with glue. Create roses using colored paper cut into small hexagons and beads or the like, and decorate the triangle with lace. Write a message in the blank area.

44

PROJECT 18
Flower Garden Sweets Box

Creator: les deux

THIS DELIGHTFUL SWEETS BOX IS SURROUNDED BY FLOWERS AND ANIMALS. SINCE YOU'LL WANT TO SHOW OFF THE BOX WHEN YOU GIVE YOUR GIFT, ENCLOSE IT IN A TRANSPARENT BAG. ONCE THE TREATS HAVE BEEN EATEN, THE BOX CAN ALSO BE USED TO HOLD SMALL TRINKETS AND JEWELRY.

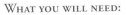

WHAT YOU WILL NEED:

- *Pressed-flower stickers (large size) / Animal motifs*
- *Thin paper / Lace paper*
- *Ribbon / Buttons / Clear vinyl bag*
- *Scissors / Glue*

1 Cover the entire box with thin paper. Then select a few pieces of lace paper that are slightly larger than the bottom of the box and glue them to the box so that they wrap around from the bottom. Use contrasting colors for the thin paper and lace papers.

2 Decorate the sides of the box with pressed-flower stickers, animal motifs, buttons, and the like. Insert a piece of lace paper into the bottom of the box and place the sweets on top of it. Insert the box into a clear bag and tie it up with ribbon.

Regularly used at patisseries in Paris, this triangular wrapping was created using a flower-patterned paper. It's perfect for wrapping tarts or quiches for a small gift to offer your host. The wrapping was finished off with grandeur by adding a pressed-flower ornament and sequins.

 What you will need:

- *Wrapping paper (wax paper or glassine paper) / Thick paper*
- *Pressed-flower stickers (large size)*
- *Thin paper / White paper*
- *Ribbon / String / Flower parts / Spangles*
- *Scissors / Cutter knife / Cutting mat / Ruler / Glue / Tape / Double-faced tape*

It's alright if the paper wrinkles when folding.

1 Cut a piece of wrapping paper into a 16-$\frac{1}{2}$ x 12 inches rectangle. Cut a piece of thick paper into a 4 x 4 inches square, and use this as a base on which to place your gift. You can adjust the sizes of the paper depending on the size of what you are going to wrap.

2 Affix the base to the center of the wrapping paper with two-sided tape. Place your gift on the base. Since the wrapping will be three-dimensional, it's all right if the gift is slightly tall.

3 As shown in the illustration, pull up both ends of the paper with your right hand and grasp them together directly above the gift. Fold one side down toward the front with your left hand to make a triangle. Then fold again toward the front to create a triangle.

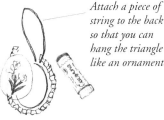

Attach a piece of string to the back so that you can hang the triangle like an ornament.

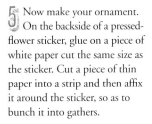

4 Fold the portion that is protruding from the base under, to the bottom, and affix it there with tape. Do the same to the other side. Then twist and gather the top, which you were grasping with your right hand.

5 Now make your ornament. On the backside of a pressed-flower sticker, glue on a piece of white paper cut the same size as the sticker. Cut a piece of thin paper into a strip and then affix it around the sticker, so as to bunch it into gathers.

6 Decorate the wrapping with flower parts or sequins and the like. Tie a strand of ribbon to the top and wrap it around the triangle wrapping with a cross shape. Pass the ribbon through the ornament and tie it into a bow at the top.

This box for decadent chocolate truffles is accentuated with a small corsage of nuanced colors like a miniature bouquet. Carefully wrapping your sweets like this is bound to send your lover's heart aflutter, making it perfect for a Valentine's gift.

What you will need:

- *Lidded box*
- *Paper corsage*
- *Flower-patterned masking tape*
- *Lace paper / Old stamps / Labels*
- *Lace / String*
- *Scissors / Glue*

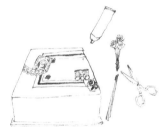

1 Create a collage on the lid of the box using masking tape, old stamps, labels, lace paper, and the like. If you limit your collage to one section, rather than covering the entire lid, your box will have a clean look.

2 Attach a corsage of miniature paper flowers. Bundle together two or three of each kind of flower, cut the stems short, and then arrange several bundles into a dome shape, and glue them on. On the box pictured to the left, about thirty flowers were used to boost the volume of the corsage.

3 Insert your gift into the box, and then wrap up the box with a string in a cross shape, and tie the string into a bow. You can create a sophisticated look by using a string that is a similar color to the box. You can also use lace to tie up your box instead of string.

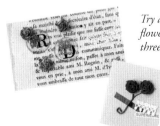

Try adding two or three small paper flowers to your card to create an elegant, three-dimensional effect.

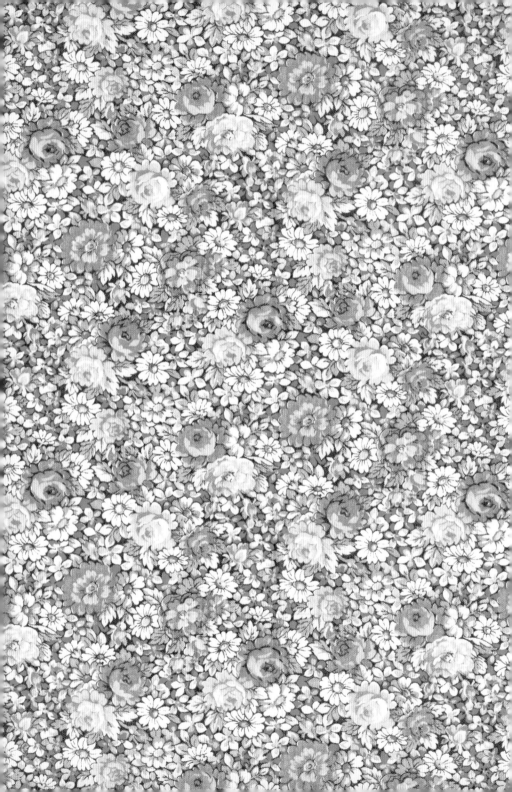

CHAPTER 3

Flowery Mini-Gifts

Of course any gift that you select for that important person in your life will be special, but sometimes it's fun to spend a little time creating a small handmade gift that's full of flowers. You can lift your spirits just by placing a few flowers in your room, and with these gifts you can do the same for your recipient.

This memo pad looks like an antique card featuring monochromatic tones contrasted with the vibrant red of an old rose. It's a cinch to make since it requires only binding with eyelets. Finished with a romantic charm, it's perfect for tucking gently into a bag.

 What you will need:

- *Thick paper / Old postcard*
- *Floral-theme stickers / Pressed flowers*
- *Clippings from an old book / Glassine paper / Lace paper / Labels*
- *Ribbon / Lace / Eyelet*
- *Needle / Embroidery thread / Eyeleter*
- *Cutter knife / Cutting mat / Ruler / Hole punch / Glue / Spray glue / Pencils / Tweezers*

1 First, make two monochrome copies of an antique postcard on colored drawing paper to create a front cover and a back cover for the memo pad. The postcard used for the pictured pad was 3 x 5 1/8 inches, but feel free to use any size you like.

2 Decorate the front cover with stickers, masking tape, labels, flower motifs, and the like. Use colorful materials to create a contrast with the monochromatic base.

3 Cut the paper for the body of the memo pad to the same size as the covers. Plain Kraft paper was used in the pictured pad. Any number of sheets can be used depending on the function, as long as the thickness can be bound with the eyelets.

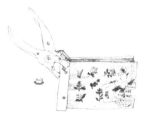

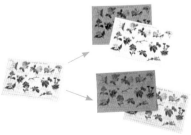

4 Cut a piece of colored drawing paper for the spine into 3 x 1 1/4 inches rectangle, and fold it in half. Layer the front cover, the pad sheets, and the back cover in that order. Insert them into the spine paper, and affix the spine paper with glue. Once dry, bind with eyelets to finish the memo pad.

The options for copying an antique postcard are varied. The top two are monochrome copies for a chic finish. The bottom two are color copies, which can yield unique effects depending on the color of paper you choose.

Perfect for a travel journal or scrapbooking, this notebook makes a great gift for a friend heading out on a trip. You can put a picture or postcard into the frame of flowers and leaves. Try selecting something unique for the body paper to give your notebook that special handmade touch.

 What you will need:

- *Thick paper (for cover) / Various types of papers (for inside pages)*
- *Flower motifs / Photographs / Photo corners*
- *String / Charms*
- *Needle / Thread / Eyeletteer*
- *Cutter knife / Cutting mat / Ruler / Glue / Stamps*

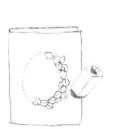

1. Cut a piece of thick paper for the cover into a 7 x 10¹/₄ inches rectangle and fold it in half. Draw a frame on the front cover part with a leaf stamp. The frame should be an oval shape that can fit the picture you'd like to insert.

2. Cut out the inside of the frame with a cutter knife, and decorate the frame with flower motifs. On the backside of the cover, affix photo corners to match the size of your picture.

3. Cut about 10 pieces of paper for the body of the notebook to match the cover's size. Fold them in half, and then insert them into the cover. Use an eyeleteer to create two holes along the fold in the center, pass a thread through the holes with a needle, and bind the notebook by knotting the thread on the inside.

4. Wrap a string twice around the spine of the notebook and tie it off, attaching a charm at one end, like the small bird above. Insert the photograph into the photo corners so that it shows through the frame on the cover.

Try using sheets with different textures than regular notebook paper, such as tracing paper or glassine paper. You can also cut the edges into a wave pattern or the like for an interesting effect.

PROJECT 23
Floral Notebook
Bound with Ribbon

Creator: Aya Nagaoka

Les fleurs

Girls love ribbons, lace, and floral patterns, and this notebook is lavishly decorated with all of them. The binding method used for this notebook is simple but sturdy. The voluminous bow creates a beautiful accent, making this notebook perfect as a guest registry for weddings or parties.

 What you will need:

- *Patterned paper (for cover) / Plain paper (for inside pages)*
- *Colored drawing paper (for title)*
- *Artificial leaves / Label plate / Ribbon*
- *Cutter knife / Cutting mat / Ruler / Eyeleteer / Glue / Pens / Tweezers*

This cross-section diagram shows the procedure for passing the ribbon.

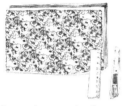

1 Cut the paper for the cover and the paper for the notebook body into 5 x 7 inches rectangles. Fold them in half once and then open them back up. Stack them up with the cover on the outside. The number of sheets for the notebook body can be adjusted according to the intended use.

2 Use an eyeleteer to make holes along the fold crease. First make one directly in the center, then make one above the center and one below the center as shown in the above illustration. Be sure to make the holes large enough to fit a piece of ribbon.

3 Pass a strand of ribbon through the holes to bind the notebook. Use tweezers if you have trouble passing the ribbon through the holes. First, pass the ribbon from the outside of hole "a" to the inside. Leave about 6 inches of the ribbon on the outside.

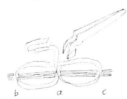

4 Next, pass the ribbon from the inside of hole "b" to the outside, and then from the outside of hole "c" to the inside. Finally, pass the ribbon from the inside of hole "a" to the outside. Tie a bow with the ribbon remaining on the outside to finish off the binding.

5 Attach a label plate to the cover and write a title. Add an accent to the label plate by decorating it with a three-dimensional motif such as a leaf for faux flowers.

PROJECT 24

Ballet Shoe Bookmark

Creator: Saji

YOU'LL LOVE TO SLIP THIS BRIGHT RED BALLET SHOE WITH ITS ADORABLE LITTLE FLOWER ORNAMENT INTO YOUR FAVORITE BOOK. THIS BEAUTIFUL BOOKMARK WILL TRANSPORT YOU INTO THE DRAMATIC WORLD OF STORIES WHENEVER YOU LIKE.

WHAT YOU WILL NEED:

- *Thick paper*
- *Drawing paper / Colored paper / Newspaper*
- *Tulle ribbon / Leather / Rhinestones / Lace motif / Clips / Charm*
- *Scissors / Glue / Brush / Paint*

1. Cut a piece of thick paper along the outside of the template below, and paint the entire piece red. Once dry, color the other side with paint as well. In the bookmark pictured, the other side is colored with an ivory paint.

Try scattering rhinestones in the center of the lace motif.

2. Cut a piece of drawing paper along the inside of the template below. Paint the entire piece ivory, and then affix it to the red piece. Cut a piece of colored paper into two thin strips and glue them on in a cross to look like the straps of the shoe.

3. Cut a piece of drawing paper into a narrow strip, form it into a loop, and glue the center together. Then cut a piece of colored paper into two small teardrop shapes and add them and a lace motif onto the loop. Affix this to the toe of the shoe.

4. On the underside, affix a piece of newspaper or leather cut to look the like sole of a ballet shoe. If you insert a clip into the sole as shown, you can clip it onto the page of a book as a bookmark. If you'd like, you can also decorate the underside of the shoe with a tulle ribbon and charm.

Ballet shoe template: enlarge by 350% (Finished size: 8 x 2¹/₄ inches)

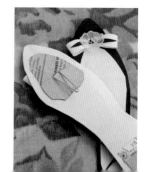

PROJECT 25

Parisian Flowers-in-Bloom Book Cover

Creator: les deux

JUST CARRYING AROUND A BOOK WITH THIS LOVELY COVER IS SURE TO PUT A SMILE ON YOUR FACE AS THE FLOWER BOOKMARKS PEEK OUT AT YOU FROM THE TOP. THE COVER COLLAGE PORTRAYS A FIELD OF FLOWERS THAT'S JUST PERFECT FOR COVERING A GUIDEBOOK TO PARIS. OFFER IT AS A GIFT TO A FRIEND ALONG WITH AN INVITATION TO TRAVEL TOGETHER.

WHAT YOU WILL NEED:

- *Patterned paper (for cover and inside cover)*
- *Labels / Flower motifs / Mini-envelope*
- *Artificial flowers with stems / Ribbon*
- *Cutter knife / Cutting mat / Ruler / Glue / Pens*

The ribbons for the bookmarks should extend from the center of the bottom side by a length that is 3/4 inch + the height of the cover.

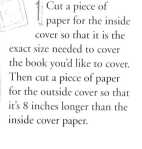

1 Cut a piece of paper for the inside cover so that it is the exact size needed to cover the book you'd like to cover. Then cut a piece of paper for the outside cover so that it's 8 inches longer than the inside cover paper.

2 Affix the outside cover paper to the inside cover paper. Put two strands of ribbon between the cover papers when affixing them to each other as shown above in the illustration. Fold over the outside cover paper that extends beyond the inside cover by 4 inches on the left and right toward the inside.

3 Attach faux flowers to the ends of the ribbons inserted between the covers. Wrap the faux stems around the ribbon and attach them with adhesive. Adjust the length so that the flowers just stick out from the top when inserted into the book.

4 Put a label with the title on the front of the book, then add flower motifs and the like. In the cover shown to the right, a miniature envelope of glassine paper was added to hold a ticket.

Try using the flower motifs you have on hand to create materials for making paper goods. For example, you can cut out the flower parts from a poster or wrapping paper. If you use special paper-cutting scissors, it will be easier to cut out the detailed portions.

PROJECT 26

Paper Carton for Your Flower Collection

Creator: les deux

flower

YELLOW RHODODENDRON
(RHODODENDRON CHRYSANTHEMUM)
(Heath Family)

Postcards, stickers of flower illustrations, floral-patterned wrapping paper—the contents of a colorful paper collection go on and on. How about gifting a friend who loves floral motifs this handmade carton to keep her collection tidy?

 What you will need:

- *Paperboard*
- *Pressed-flower stickers*
- *Patterned paper / White paper (for the photocopy) / Butterfly motifs*
- *Book cloth / Lace doily (for the photocopy) / Miniature dollhouse frame / Ribbon / Lace*
- *Scissors / Cutter knife / Cutting mat / Ruler / Glue / Pens*

You can use a color copy of a plain fabric on paper instead of the book cloth.

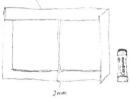

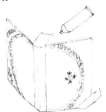

1 Cut two pieces of paperboard into 10 5/16 x 8 inches rectangles. Cut a piece of book cloth into a 13 x 18 inches rectangle, then align the two pieces of paperboard in the center and affix them with glue. Fold the protruding book cloth so as to wrap it over the paperboard and affix it with glue.

2 Color copy an antique doily, cut it out, and affix it to the front cover of the carton. Affix a wide ribbon onto the spine and the four corners. Fold over the protruding parts of the ribbon and affix them to the inside.

3 Cut a piece of patterned paper into a 10 x 15 inches rectangle and affix it to the inside of the carton, so as to cover up the book cloth and the ends of the ribbon that you folded onto the inside. A colorful pattern will give your carton a lively feel.

When cutting the ends of the lace, leave about 10 inches on each end to use for tying up and closing the carton.

4 Affix strands of lace to form a border along the four edges of the patterned paper. Be sure to firmly affix the lace so that the patterned paper does not peel off.

5 Lay a strand of lace across the inside of the carton for holding papers or the like, and attach it with adhesive at only the center and the two ends. A stretchy lace will provide a sturdy hold when using the carton.

6 Finally, decorate the cover. Put the title in a mini-frame and scatter pressed-flower stickers, butterfly motifs, and the like. Decorate the back cover in a similar way.

PROJECT 27

Card Case with
Floral Brooch

Creator: Aya Nagaoka

This chic and sophisticated card case is embellished with a collage of flower motifs in subdued color tones and an interesting accessory like a brooch. When you open the flap, a floral pattern blooms in front of your eyes like a sweeping field of flowers. A friend embarking on a new career will appreciate this lovely gift.

 What you will need:

- *Thick paper*
- *Flower-patterned paper*
- *Pressed-flower stickers*
- *Clippings from an old book / Labels / Flower motifs*
- *Lace / Brooch base / Snap button*
- *Needle / Thread / Eyeleteer*
- *Cutter knife / Cutting mat / Ruler / Glue*

Cut a pressed-flower sticker to the same size as the brooch base and then fit it into the brooch.

1 Affix a flower motif paper to a piece of thick paper, and then cut it using the template below. Run the back of a cutter knife along the dotted line parts to make fold creases, and then fold up the paper along the creases to create the card case.

2 Attach a snap button on the flap portion so that the case can be firmly closed. Once you've chosen a spot, make a hole for passing through a needle with an eyeleteer, and sew on the snap button with a thread. Sew on the button receiver in the same way.

3 Decorate the flap portion with a collage of cutouts from old books, labels, flower motifs, lace, and the like. Insert a pressed-flower sticker onto a brooch base and attach it to the flap for a finishing touch.

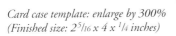

Card case template: enlarge by 300%
(Finished size: $2^5/_{16}$ x 4 x $^1/_4$ inches)

THIS CLASSICAL FRAME, LIKE ONE YOU MIGHT FIND IN AN OLD EUROPEAN MANSION, IS FESTOONED WITH A LUSCIOUS ROSE CORSAGE. LIKE A MAGICAL SPELL, THIS PAPER FRAME CAN TRANSFORM AN ORDINARY SNAPSHOT INTO A WORK OF ART. TRY MAKING YOUR OWN SMALL PHOTO GALLERY BY CREATING SEVERAL FRAMES OF DIFFERENT SIZES AND DISPLAYING THEM ALONG A WALL.

1. Using any frame you have on hand, make a color copy of the frame on drawing paper, adjusting the size to match the picture you'd like to use. Feel free to adjust the size and shade of color to your liking. Cut out the inside of the frame with a cutter knife.

2. Affix a piece of thick paper on the back surface of the drawing paper, and press them together by sticking them into a dictionary or other thick book until they are completely dry. This will give your frame a flat finish with no warping.

3. Cut out the affixed papers along the outside of the frame, cutting off any extra portions around the frame. Cut out the inside of the frame leaving about 2 inches of the thick paper part on each side as shown in the illustration.

This photo frame features a three-dimensional texture so realistic that you'll hardly believe it's made of paper. These photos were fitted with black-and-white pictures for a classical finish.

- *Drawing paper / Thick paper (black or dark colored)*
- *Paper corsage*
- *Photographs / Old stamps*
- *Frame (for the photocopy) / Artificial leaves / Expanded sheet*
- *Scissors / Cutter knife / Cutting mat / Ruler / Glue*

4 Decorate the frame with antique stamps, lace, or the like to complement your picture. Be sure to leave space for your paper corsage when decorating the frame.

5 Flip over the frame, cut two narrow strips of a foam sheet, and affix them to the top and bottom on the inside of the frame. Then attach your picture on top of these strips. This will provide three-dimensionality and depth to your frame.

6 In the space left over, attach a paper corsage with leaves from faux flowers. The trick to achieving a good balance is to not be afraid of using a large corsage.

Corsages that you'll find for sale in stores come in a variety of materials, such as paper, fabric, and even tree bark. Try using them in your flower corsages to enhance their individuality and design.

THIS SOFTLY SCENTED SACHET WAS MADE BY ENCASING
FRAGRANT POTPOURRI INSIDE LACE PAPER, AND ACCENTING
WITH A DAINTY LILY OF THE VALLEY. IT'S LOVELY TO LOOK AT
WHEN ADORNED IN A ROOM LIKE AN ORNAMENT.

 WHAT YOU WILL NEED:

• *Lace paper*
• *Flower-patterned masking tape*
• *Labels / Flower motifs*
• *Dried lily of the valley / Potpourri / Lace / Beads / Charm / Non-woven cloth*
• *Needle / Thread*
• *Scissors / Glue / Sealing stamps / Sealing wax*

1 Cut two pieces of non-woven fabric into circles to match the center circle of the lace paper you will use. Sew up the edges around $3/4$ of the perimeter, then insert a small amount of potpourri and sew up the remaining $1/4$.

2 Stack two circles of the lace paper so that the backs are facing each other, and then sew them together along the portions with holes as shown in the illustration. Sew up the edges around $3/4$ of the perimeter, then insert the potpourri pouch and sew up the remaining $1/4$.

3 Decorate the sachet with a collage of masking tape, flower motifs, lace, beads, and the like. Attach a dried lily of the valley with a label, and then affix a piece of lace for hanging the sash using sealing wax.

Lace paper is a must-have item when making collages. In addition to white, you can collect various sizes and colors like red, pink, and brown and combine them in any way you can imagine.

PROJECT 30

Nostalgic
Mercerie Box

Creator: les deux

This mercerie box provides a nostalgic aura, but it's more than just a pretty decoration. The top is actually a convenient fluffy pin cushion. Try filling it with color threads and lace and gifting it to a craft-loving friend.

 What you will need:

- *Thick paper / Cloth*
- *Colored paper / Dollhouse lace motifs (ribbon type)*
- *Ribbon / Cotton*
- *Scissors / Cutter knife / Cutting mat / Ruler / Glue / Double-faced tape / Compasses*

For the strip of lace motif, you can substitute actual lace with an enlarged color copy of an antique lace or tyrolean tape.

Affix a strand of ribbon onto the boundary line between the pin cushion and the side surface of the lid.

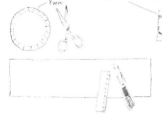

1 First make the lid. Cut a piece of thick paper into a 2 x 10 5/16 inches long rectangle, and a circle with a 4 inches diameter. Make small cuts of about 5/16 inch around the outer perimeter of the circle as shown in the illustration above.

2 Affix a lace motif to the rectangle and cut off any protruding edges. Fashion the rectangle into a ring and fix it with two-sided tape. Fold down the cut parts around the edges of the circle, and then fit it onto the ring and seal it with glue.

3 Now create the pin cushion. Cut a piece of fabric into a circle of 5 1/2 inches in diameter, and make small cuts of about 1/4 inch around the outer perimeter of the circle. Affix the circle onto the top surface of the box. Once you've affixed about half of the perimeter, stuff the pin cushion with cotton and then seal the rest of the perimeter.

4 Next, make the box portion in the same way as the lid. Cut a piece of thick paper into a 2 x 10 inches long rectangle, and a circle of 3 3/4 inches in diameter. Affix a strip of colored paper onto the long rectangle and fashion it into a ring. Then make cuts on the circle, fold them over, and fit the circle onto the ring to make the box bottom.

Instead of a pin cushion, you can decorate the top of the lid with floral motifs and lace paper to make a gift box. This would also make a handy box to collect lace or buttons.

Artist Profiles

les deux
Mihoko Takimura
Miyuki Matsuo

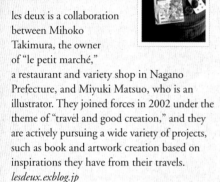

les deux is a collaboration between Mihoko Takimura, the owner of "le petit marché," a restaurant and variety shop in Nagano Prefecture, and Miyuki Matsuo, who is an illustrator. They joined forces in 2002 under the theme of "travel and good creation," and they are actively pursuing a wide variety of projects, such as book and artwork creation based on inspirations they have from their travels. *lesdeux.exblog.jp*

Saji
Miki Sajima

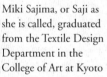

Miki Sajima, or Saji as she is called, graduated from the Textile Design Department in the College of Art at Kyoto Seika University in Japan, and is currently working as a freelance illustrator. Saji creates artwork with her own unique methods, such as cutouts and collages using unique kinds of paper as a base. While actively contributing her work to advertising campaigns and magazines, she also regularly enters her designs in exhibitions. *www.sajimart.net*

Ananö
Rie Mizoe

Rie Mizoe began creating her unique tiny bears and other fabric crafts in 1997, and established her company, Ananö, in 2001. Beginning with products under the theme "crafting with a unique touch," Ananö quickly established a reputation for its high quality crafts, and has since gone on to create a number of books, which Mizoe fully produces on her own—from the photography and styling to the illustrations. She is also active in character design. *www.anano.net*

Aya Nagaoka

As an editor and craft planner, Aya Nagaoka creates scrapbooks and collages accented by antique European paper goods such as antique cards, vintage stamps, and scrap pictures. She is the author of numerous books such as *Sukurappuhorikku no Hon* ("The Scrapholic's Book"), *Masukingu Tepu de Koraju* ("Making Collages by Masking Tape"), and *Furenchi Koraju Ressun* ("French Collage Lesson").

Styling cooperation

Orné de Feuilles
1F Aoyama O bldg., 2-3-3 Shibuya
Shibuya-ku, Tokyo 150-0002, Japan
Tel +81 (3) 3499-0140

AWABEES
3-50-11-5F Sendagaya
Shibuya-ku, Tokyo 151-0051, Japan
Tel +81 (3) 5786-1600

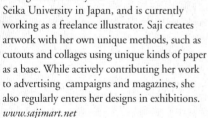

Flower Motif Collection for Crafting

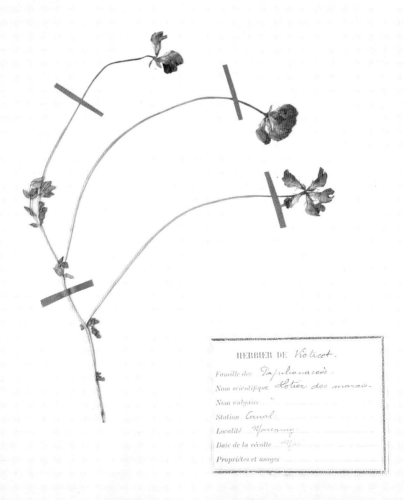

HERBIER DE *Violicot.*

Famille des *Papilionacées*.
Nom scientifique *Lotier des marais.*
Nom vulgaire ... "
Station *Canal.*
Localité *Montagne.*
Date de la récolte *Mai*
Propriétés et usages

A B C D E F

G H I J K

L M N O P

Q R S T U

V W X Y Z

Numbers

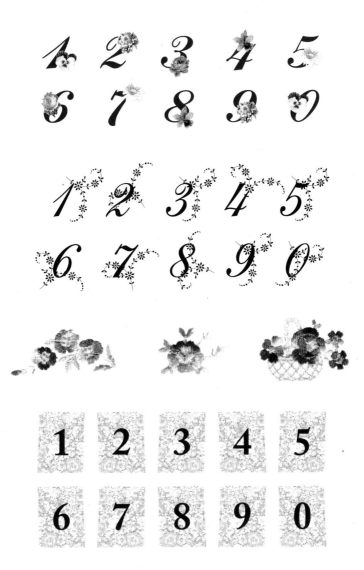

Motifs

LABELS

Buttons

LACE AND RIBBONS

Flower decals

Pressed flowers

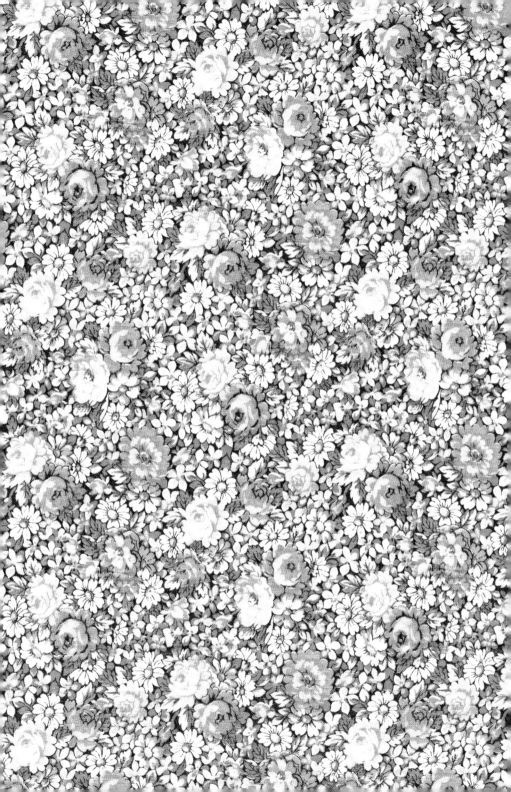

ande richesse d'exécution. Elle est
, dans lesquels sont disposées les

broderie, richelieu, passé plat, an-

, pur fil, prendre du *Coton à Broder*

Brillanté C-B « A la Croix » Cartier-Bresson, à 1 fr. l'éch
la toile de lin bise ou la toile de Rhodes bise, prendre
Croix » Cartier-Bresson, art. 219, n° 5, en gris toile 578, la
4 : 32 fr. 75. Pour la toile de Rhodes crème, du *Perlé écru*
les 4 : 28 fr. 75.

(*Voir la suite des*

A 953

A 947

A 956

A 948

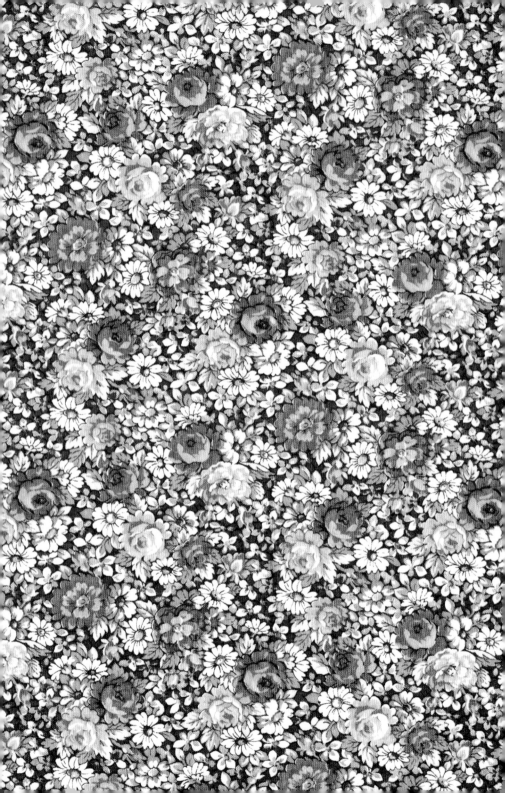